A WORD IN SEASON

A Collection of Forty Inspiring Lessons

BY ISAAC SAMUEL II

DEDICATION

With deep gratitude and heartfelt appreciation, I dedicate this book to all of you—the remarkable members of our beloved church whose unwavering support, dedication, and active involvement have touched my heart. As your pastor, it is an immense honor to serve alongside every one of you, and I am humbled by the privilege of sharing this extraordinary faith journey with you.

A wise person once said, "A leader without followers is only taking a walk." Through your tireless commitment and wholehearted participation, you have become my invaluable companions on this purposeful path. Like the Berean church in the book of Acts, you have embraced the Word with open minds and diligently searched the Scriptures daily. Your hunger for truth and eagerness to live out the teachings of Christ inspire me beyond words.

Check It Church International is more than a place of worship; it is a vibrant global community. Our online congregation, spanning continents and time zones, has proven that distance cannot diminish the power of our unity in Christ. Together, we stand as a testament to the boundless reach of the Gospel and the transformative power of God's love.

My prayer is that this book will serve as a cherished reminder of the incredible journey we have embarked upon together. May it provide you with ongoing inspiration and guidance as you continue to walk in faith. Let it stand as a powerful testimony to the remarkable achievements we can accomplish when we live in the atmosphere of God's Word, God's Worship, and God's Miracles.

PREFACE

Welcome to "A Word in Season," a collection of forty uplifting lessons written by Pastor Isaac Samuel II. This book will take you on a journey of transformation, exploring various topics that will encourage deep thought and strengthen your faith as a Christian.

As you read through these pages, you will discover valuable insights, meaningful stories, and practical wisdom rooted in the timeless truths of the Scriptures. Pastor Isaac Samuel II warmly invites you to explore these lessons with an open heart and a desire to embrace the transformative power of God's Word.

May this book inspire and motivate you in your spiritual growth. May its teachings draw you closer to the heart of a loving God who is always by your side. As you face life's challenges, may you find unwavering faith and reassurance in knowing you are never alone. May you experience the richness of God's Word, God's Worship, and God's Miracles in Jesus' Name. Amen.

CONTENTS

01. God Is Doing a New Thing 7

02. Tap Into The Wells of Salvation 11

03. The Blood Makes You Untouchable 15

04. God Forgives and Forgets Our Sins 19

05. The Power of Rejoicing 23

06. God, The Extraordinary Strategist 27

07. Unveiling the Power of Prayer 31

08. Rising to Walk in Restoration 35

09. Seeds of Transformation 39

10. The Proof of Love 43

11. The Liberating Power of the Anointing 47

12. A Celebration of God's Masterpiece 52

13. Choosing Our Battles Wisely 56

14. You Are Special to God 60

15. Discovering Your True Identity 64

16. The Fragrance of Divine Favor 69

17. The Assurance of Victory 73

18. The Danger of Exalting Ourselves 77

19. Declared Not Guilty 81

20. Enjoying the Blessings of the Covenant 85

21. The Rewards of Giving Jesus Your Boat 89

22. Having Something to Multiply 93

23. The Victorious Path of Faith 97

24. Striving for Contentment 101

25. Liberation Through the Truth 105

26. Forgiveness is a Choice 109

27. Living with Diplomatic Immunity 113

28. Seeking a Sign 117

29. Boasting in the Lord 121

30. The Heart of Worship 125

31. Submitting to His Will 129

32. The Dynamic Trio 133

33. Praying for God's Sent Leaders 137

34. Steadfast in Purpose 141

35. Becoming People After God's Heart 145

36. Nurturing a Positive Mindset 149

37. Fighting the Good Fight 153

38. Pray For Your Country 157

39. A Strong Tower 161

40. The Promise of Rest 165

CHAPTER 1
GOD IS DOING A NEW THING

---

*"Behold, I will do a new thing; now it shall spring forth;
shall ye not know it? I will even make a way in the
wilderness, and rivers in the desert."*
Isaiah 43:19

Imagine a desert that is dry and lifeless, where not even a single cactus flower can grow. Now picture that same desert transforming into a vibrant oasis, with bubbling pools of water bringing life and beauty. In Isaiah 43:19, God assures us that He is doing something completely new in our lives. He is making a way through seemingly impossible situations and causing a stream to flow through the barren wilderness. In simpler terms, God is promising to do amazing things and provide refreshing solutions even in the most challenging and hopeless circumstances.

Today, I want to encourage you by reminding you that God has a special plan for your life. His love for you is unwavering, and nothing can come between you and His love. No matter what obstacles you face, remember that God is greater, and He will help you overcome them. Stay confident and hopeful as you move forward.

In Proverbs 4:18, it says that the path of the righteous is like a shining light that becomes brighter and brighter until the perfect day. You are on the right path, and your future is filled with brightness. Keep shining and growing. The challenges you encounter are steppingstones on your journey to success.

You are like an unstoppable and powerful train. With God on your side, nothing can stand against you. He will deliver you, defend you, and provide for you. Fear nothing, for God's love for you is unconditional and unwavering.

If you were feeling down before, know that God's love is always ready to uplift you. Trust in Him, and He will give you the strength and courage to conquer any challenge.

Remember, you are never alone. God is constantly watching over you, guiding you, and protecting you. Your future is bright, and your success is certain. With God by your side, there is no limit to what you can achieve. Take heart and believe in yourself, for you are destined for greatness. God is doing something new and wonderful in your life!

REFLECTION

CHAPTER 2
TAP INTO THE WELLS OF SALVATION

"Therefore, with joy shall ye draw water out of the wells of salvation."
Isaiah 12:3

Life can be tough, but it's important to remember that we can find joy even in the hardest times. According to Habakkuk 3:17-19 and Isaiah 12:3, there's a source of hope, healing, and happiness within us called the wells of salvation. But how do we access these wells?

Fortunately, the Bible tells us that we can tap into them by rejoicing. James 1:2-3 and Romans 4:18-22 teach us that rejoicing in difficult times is crucial because it helps us connect with the wells of salvation inside us. By trusting in God's promises and finding joy in Him, we can overcome any challenge. Even if we can't see how God will fulfill His promises, we can have faith that He will support and guide us through every obstacle.

When we face trials and challenges, we can confuse the devil by rejoicing and drawing from the water that brings true happiness, and peace of mind. This way, we can be sure that the devil's plans won't succeed, and he will eventually go away.

Rejoicing also holds a special power—it invites angels into our lives. When we tap into the wells of Salvation and genuinely experience joy, we create an atmosphere that attracts these celestial beings. Angels are drawn to our happiness and celebration, and in their presence, they bring blessings and messages from God.

Always remember that everything you need can be found in the wells of salvation. So, keep your faith strong and hold on to the hope that comes from trusting and rejoicing in the Lord. As Psalm 46:1 says, "God is our refuge and strength, a very present help in trouble." God will sustain and guide us through every obstacle, but we need to tap into the wells of Salvation to overcome. So, let's always rejoice in the Lord and find joy in every situation. With God on our side, we can overcome any challenge and come out stronger and happier than ever.

REFLECTION

CHAPTER 3

THE BLOOD MAKES YOU UNTOUCHABLE

"For God so loved the world, that he gave his only begotten Son, that whosoever believeth in him should not perish, but have everlasting life."
John 3:16

Dear brothers and sisters, let us rejoice in the wonderful truth that we are protected and safe through the precious blood of Jesus Christ. In John 3:16, we are reminded of God's immense love for us, and the sacrifice Jesus made to give us eternal life. This knowledge should fill our minds with heavenly thoughts, knowing that our lives are securely hidden with Christ in God (Colossians 3:2-4). We can find peace and assurance, knowing that we are in God's loving hands.

Just like Mordecai in the book of Esther, we too are shielded from harm when we have faith in God. When Haman tried to hurt Mordecai, he failed because Mordecai was of Jewish descent, and his faith protected him. Even Haman's own advisors and his wife told him that he would not succeed against Mordecai. Esther 6:12-14 reminds us that God is our refuge and fortress, and no weapon formed against us will succeed. We can take comfort in the fact that God protects us, and we are invincible with Him.

We should also remember that God qualifies us and gives us the ability to do things. 2 Corinthians 3:5 and Philippians 4:13 reminds us that we can't achieve anything on our own, but with God's help, we can do all things. Therefore, let us trust in God and have faith in His power. His blood speaks for us and makes us unconquerable. With God as our ally, we can overcome any challenge and come out stronger than before.

So, let us stay positive and comforted, knowing that we are untouchable and secure in the love of Christ. Let us trust in God's provision and recognize Him as our protector and defender. With God on our side, we can face anything with courage and confidence, knowing that we are unbeatable in Him.

REFLECTION

CHAPTER 4
GOD FORGIVES AND FORGETS OUR SINS

"I, even I, am he that blotteth out thy transgressions for mine own sake and will not remember thy sins."
Isaiah 43:25

Many believers often feel overwhelmed by the difficulties they face in life, such as money problems, sickness, and other heavy burdens. But there is hope in a story from the Bible, Luke 13:11-14, which tells us about a woman who had been bent over by a spirit of sickness for eighteen years. When she met Jesus, her life was changed forever.

Jesus saw the woman and called her to Him. He said, "Woman, you are free from your sickness." He touched her, and right away she stood up straight and praised God. The religious leader in the synagogue was upset because Jesus had healed her on the Sabbath, a day of rest. But Jesus reminded him that even on the Sabbath, people untie their animals to give them water. Shouldn't this woman, who is a part of God's family, be released from her burden on the Sabbath?

This story shows us that Jesus is ready and able to free us from our burdens, no matter how long we have carried them. In Galatians 3:29, it says that if we belong to Jesus, we are part of God's special people and receive His promises. He has saved us, called us by name, and promised to be with us through all the challenges of life.

In Isaiah 43:1-7, God promises to be with us in every difficulty, protecting and guiding us. He reminds us that He is our Savior and that He loves us. In Isaiah 43:17-19, we see that God can do new things in our lives, even when it seems impossible.

Lastly, in Isaiah 43:25, we learn that God forgives our sins and forgets them. We should not dwell on what God has already forgiven us for. It is the devil who tries to remind us of our past sins, but we can reject his lies because he is a deceiver.

Let us bring our burdens to Jesus and lay them down before Him. He is ready and able to free us from our burdens and give us new life and hope. By trusting in His promises and His love for us, we can find peace and rest even in the midst of life's challenges.

REFLECTION

CHAPTER 5
THE POWER OF REJOICING

"Rejoice in the Lord alway: and again I say, Rejoice."
Philippians 4:4

Today, I want to remind you about the incredible power of joy and praise. Life can be difficult and overwhelming, but when we choose to rejoice, something amazing happens. It changes the atmosphere around us. The heaviness and burdens we carry begin to lift, and we find freedom and peace.

In Isaiah 61:1-3, we are reminded that the Spirit of the Lord is upon us. He has anointed us to bring good news and comfort to those who are hurting. We can exchange our sorrow for joy and put on a garment of praise. It's like being planted as righteous trees by the Lord Himself.

When the people of Judah faced a powerful enemy, they cried out to God for help. God responded, saying, "Do not be afraid or discouraged... for the battle is not yours, but God's" (2 Chronicles 20:15). They were instructed to appoint singers who would praise the beauty of holiness. As they sang and praised, the Lord caused confusion among their enemies. Singing and praising can be a powerful weapon in spiritual battles.

Even Jesus Himself sang and rejoiced. After the Last Supper, Jesus and His disciples sang a hymn together (Matthew 26:30). In Luke 10:21, we see that Jesus rejoiced in spirit and gave thanks to the Father.

So, I want to encourage you to let go of sadness and heaviness and embrace the oil of joy and the garment of praise. Let us sing and rejoice because the battle belongs to the Lord. He is always with us, fighting for us. May we follow the example of the people of Judah and place our trust in God, witnessing His victory in our lives. And may we follow the example of Jesus, who sang and rejoiced in every circumstance.

Take heart, my friend. The oil of joy has been poured out upon you. Rejoice in the Lord always, and once again I say, rejoice!

REFLECTION

CHAPTER 6
GOD, THE EXTRAORDINARY STRATEGIST

"Trust in the LORD with all thine heart; and lean not unto thine own understanding. In all thy ways acknowledge him, and he shall direct thy paths."
Proverbs 3:5-6

Have you ever found yourself in a situation where you feel trapped with no way out? Maybe you're facing a huge challenge that seems impossible to overcome, and you're feeling hopeless. In moments like these, it's important to remember that God always has a plan. He is an incredible strategist, and He knows exactly what to do in every situation.

The Bible is full of examples that show God's strategic thinking. One well-known story is when Jesus fed the 5,000 people. The disciples were worried because they didn't have enough food, but Jesus had a plan. He took a small offering of five loaves of bread and two fish from a boy, thanked God for it, and miraculously fed the entire crowd with plenty of food left over! This story teaches us that God can take something small and turn it into something amazing.

Another example is the Battle of Jericho. When Joshua was told to conquer the city of Jericho, God gave him a unique strategy. The Israelites were instructed to march around the city walls for six days. Then, on the seventh day, they were to march around the city seven times while the priests blew their trumpets. Finally, they were to shout, and the walls of Jericho would collapse. It may have seemed strange, but they trusted God's plan, and it worked!

The Exodus from Egypt is another incredible example of God's strategic planning. He led Moses in freeing the Israelites from slavery, using a series of plagues to convince Pharaoh to let them go. And when they left Egypt, God had a plan to protect them from the pursuing Egyptian army. He parted the Red Sea, allowing the Israelites to cross on dry land. But when the Egyptians tried to follow, the sea closed back up, saving the Israelites, and defeating their enemies.

Lastly, consider the story of Gideon's army. When Gideon was chosen to lead the Israelites against the Midianites, God instructed him to reduce the size of his army significantly. Through a series of tests, God selected only a small group of soldiers. With this smaller force, Gideon was able to surprise and defeat the much larger Midianite army. It showed that victory depended on faith and obedience to God, not just sheer numbers.

So, my friend, take heart. If you're feeling trapped and hopeless, remember that God always has a plan. He is an amazing strategist who can use even the most unlikely people and resources to accomplish His purposes. Trust in Him, and He will guide you through even the most challenging situations.

REFLECTION

CHAPTER 7
UNVEILING THE POWER OF PRAYER

"Is any among you afflicted? let him pray. Is any merry? let him sing psalms."
James 5:13

Prayer is a powerful tool that can transform our lives and the world around us. It allows us to connect with God, experience His love and grace, and receive guidance and understanding from the Holy Spirit. Through prayer, we can overcome challenges and fulfill our purpose in life.

In the book of James, we are reminded that prayer is essential in all circumstances. When we are facing difficulties, we can turn to God in prayer for comfort and deliverance. And when we are joyful, we can express our gratitude through praise and worship. Prayer brings us closer to God and fills the void in our hearts that only He can satisfy.

Looking at the story of Daniel, we see the impact of fervent prayer. Daniel's prayers brought him divine visitations and understanding beyond his own capabilities. The Holy Spirit imparted wisdom and insight, enabling Daniel to navigate complex situations. Our prayers can also unlock supernatural wisdom and abilities as we connect with God and seek His guidance.

The account of Moses encountering an angel in the burning bush illustrates how angels are sent by God to fulfill His purposes. Angels provide assistance and empowerment, helping us fulfill our destinies and become agents of change in the world.

Even Jesus Himself experienced angelic intervention when He prayed in the garden of Gethsemane. An angel appeared to strengthen Him in His time of need. This serves as a reminder that when we are going through trials and burdens, our prayers summon the help of angels, bringing us strength and comfort.

It's important to note that we do not worship angels. They are messengers sent by God to support and encourage us. When we receive insights or promptings from Scripture, it may be the work of angels under the guidance of the Holy Spirit. That's why it is valuable to keep our Bibles close and seek God's wisdom through prayer.

As we deepen our prayer lives and align ourselves with God's purposes, we can expect angelic assistance along our faith journey. Let us cherish the gift of prayer and remain open to the supernatural workings of God. Trust that He will send His angels to strengthen, guide, and empower us every step of the way.

REFLECTION

CHAPTER 8
RISING TO WALK IN RESTORATION

---

*"...I will put none of these diseases upon thee,
which I have brought upon the Egyptians: for
I am the LORD that healeth thee."*
Exodus 15:26

Today, I want to share with you a special name of God that reveals an important part of who He is. In Exodus 15:26, God introduces Himself as "The Lord Who Heals You." Healing is not just something God does from time to time; it is a fundamental part of His character. Throughout the Bible, we see Jesus healing the sick, restoring the broken, and bringing wholeness to those in need. Why does He do this? The answer is simple: Jesus heals because it is His nature, and He has deep compassion for people.

In John 5, there is a powerful story that takes place at the Pool of Bethesda. Jesus comes across a man who has been paralyzed for a long time and asks him a life-changing question: "Do you want to be made well?" This seemingly simple question carries great significance. It stirs up faith in the man and opens the door for his miraculous healing. The man believed that he could be healed and desired it with all his heart. He was ready to take action and walk in that healing without making excuses.

Today, Jesus is asking each one of us the same question: "Do you want to be made well?" He is calling us to rise above our brokenness and embrace the restoration that He offers. Whether it's physical healing, financial breakthrough, or the restoration of relationships, Jesus invites us to respond with faith and surrender. When we answer His call, He not only brings healing but also empowers us to fulfill our God-given purpose with strength and courage.

It's important to remember that healing does not always happen instantly; it can be a process. Just like the man at the Pool of Bethesda, we may need to take steps of faith and trust in God's timing. Not every healing occurs in a moment, but we can hold onto the promise that God is the Lord who heals us. He is with us every step of the way, guiding us, strengthening us, and transforming us.

Let us give glory to God for His healing power and embrace the journey of restoration. As we walk in faith, let us rely on the assurance that God is faithful to His word. He is the Lord who heals us, and He is actively working in us and through us. May our lives be a testimony to His healing touch, and may we experience His transformative power in every area of our lives.

REFLECTION

CHAPTER 9
SEEDS OF TRANSFORMATION

"For all the promises of God in him are yea, and in him
Amen, unto the glory of God by us."
2 Corinthians 1:20

God's promises are like powerful seeds of transformation and restoration found in His Word. These promises have the ability to reshape our lives, but we have a responsibility to nurture and believe in them, just as a gardener tends to a seed.

Sometimes, we may question how and when God will fulfill His promises. However, we must trust in His infinite wisdom and control over all things. He knows exactly how to bring His promises to pass in our lives. Instead of becoming impatient or doubtful, we should surrender ourselves to His divine will and have faith that He will provide everything necessary for His promises to come true. God's timing is perfect, and His ways are beyond our comprehension.

Our response to God's promises is crucial in their fulfillment. The story of the Israelites in Deuteronomy 1:19-45 serves as a reminder that doubt, disobedience, and lack of faith can hinder God's plans for us. As we wait for His promises to be realized, we must align ourselves with His truth, walking in faith and obedience. We need to guard our hearts against doubt and unbelief, choosing to trust in God's unwavering faithfulness.

Similar to how a seed needs the right conditions to grow and bear fruit, we must create an environment that fosters the fulfillment of God's promises. This involves saturating our minds with His Word, surrounding ourselves with a community of believers who uplift and support us, and cultivating a lifestyle of prayer and worship. In this fertile ground of faith, the seeds of God's promises take root and flourish.

Always remember that God's promises are not empty words. They possess the power to transform lives and bring about restoration. As we faithfully nurture these promises with unwavering belief, we can trust that God will bring them to fruition in His perfect timing. Let us embrace the role of faithful gardeners, tending to the seeds of God's promises and eagerly anticipating the bountiful harvest that awaits us.

REFLECTION

CHAPTER 10
THE PROOF OF LOVE

"Greater love hath no man than this, that a man lay down his life for his friends."
John 15:13

Love is the foundation of the Christian faith, embodying God's character and forming the core of our relationship with Him. The Apostle Paul emphasizes the importance of love in 1 Corinthians 13:13, placing it above faith and hope. Love is more than mere sentiment; it is a powerful force that moves us to give and forgive.

Jesus exemplified love through His actions during His time on Earth. In Matthew 11:4-5, He instructed John the Baptist's disciples to witness the miracles He performed—restoring sight to the blind, enabling the lame to walk, cleansing lepers, healing the deaf, raising the dead, and preaching the gospel to the poor. These acts of compassion demonstrated God's love in action.

To truly understand love, we must embody it. Ephesians 3:19 urges us to comprehend the immeasurable love of Christ, going beyond knowledge and being filled with the fullness of God. Love is not merely a concept; it is meant to be experienced and expressed in our daily lives. When we truly grasp God's unwavering love for us and how valued we are in His eyes, it compels us to extend that love to others.

So, how do we show love? Firstly, we must genuinely believe in God's unconditional love for us. Secondly, we must walk in love, allowing it to guide our thoughts, words, and actions. Love should motivate everything we do. Lastly, love involves giving and forgiving. Giving is a natural outpouring of love as we share our time, resources, and abilities with others. Forgiving is also essential, as we choose to release bitterness and show mercy to those who have wronged us.

Love is not just empty words; it is demonstrated through giving and forgiving. As Christians, we are called to reflect the love of Christ, allowing it to permeate every aspect of our lives. Let us strive to walk in love, generously giving and wholeheartedly forgiving, thereby showcasing God's love in action. In doing so, we bring hope, healing, and transformation to those around us, revealing the profound power of God's love.

REFLECTION

CHAPTER 11
THE LIBERATING POWER OF THE ANOINTING

"How God anointed Jesus of Nazareth with the Holy Ghost and with power: who went about doing good, and healing all that were oppressed of the devil; for God was with him."
Acts 10:38

The anointing of the Holy Spirit is like a never-ending well of power and authority. It is a precious gift given to believers, offering hope, healing, deliverance, and freedom to all who seek it. Throughout Jesus Christ's life and ministry, we witnessed the incredible impact of this anointing as He walked the earth, reaching out His hands to heal the sick, free the oppressed, and release people from their chains.

In Acts 10:38, we are reminded of the remarkable anointing that rested upon Jesus. God anointed Jesus of Nazareth with the Holy

Spirit and power, and He went around doing good and healing all who were under the devil's oppression. This anointing was not limited by time or place; it flowed freely, touching those in desperate need.

A striking example of the anointing's power can be seen in the encounter between Jesus and the Samaritan woman at the well, described in John 4:4-42. Through His prophetic anointing, Jesus supernaturally located her, seeing beyond her outward appearance and into the depths of her soul. He broke the curse of her troubled relationships, bringing about a profound transformation and freedom. The anointing's discernment and revelation shattered the chains that held her captive, offering a fresh start and a new hope.

Likewise, the story of the Madman of Gadarenes in Mark 5 demonstrates how the anointing brings deliverance to those tormented and oppressed. With compassion and authority, Jesus used the anointing of deliverance to free this tormented soul from demonic possession. The anointing's power shattered the chains that bound the man, restoring his sanity, purpose, and dignity. It is a powerful example of the liberation that can be experienced through the anointing of the Holy Spirit.

Beyond healing and deliverance, the anointing has the power to break every chain that seeks to imprison us. Acts 16:24-26 tells the inspiring story of Paul and Silas, imprisoned for their faith. In the midst of their dire circumstances, they chose to pray and sing hymns to God, activating the anointing's power through their unwavering faith. Suddenly, a mighty earthquake shook the prison, opening the doors and loosening the prisoners' chains. It was a remarkable display of God's intervention and the breaking of physical restraints through the anointing's mighty influence.

These illustrations of the anointing's power remind us of a profound truth: "The yoke has been broken because of the anointing." As believers, we have been empowered by the anointing of the Holy Spirit, equipped with authority and power to break free from burdens, limitations, and strongholds that hinder our progress. Just as Jesus demonstrated during His earthly ministry, we are entrusted with the responsibility to do good, heal the sick, deliver the oppressed, and break every yoke that tries to hold us back. The anointing of God's Spirit rests upon us, enabling us to live lives of freedom, purpose, and transformation. Let us embrace this anointing and allow its living waters to flow through us, bringing hope and deliverance to a world in need.

REFLECTION

CHAPTER 12

A CELEBRATION OF GOD'S MASTERPIECE

"But even the very hairs of your head are all numbered. Fear not therefore: ye are of more value than many sparrows."
Luke 12:7

Years ago, as a young child, I asked my mom, "Did Prince Charles and Lady Diana have the greatest wedding ever?" Her answer surprised me as she confidently replied, "No!"

Baffled by her response, I couldn't comprehend why she would say that when I had heard their wedding was hailed the "wedding of the century."

Curious, I asked, "Then which wedding was the best?" Anticipating a mention of some royal affair in a distant European land, I was taken aback when she simply said, "Mine." Given the grandeur associated with Prince Charles and Lady Diana's nuptials, I couldn't understand her reasoning.

Later, she explained something profound to me. She said that everyone has their own perspective and personal preferences. What was most memorable and special to her was her own wedding day.

As I've grown older, I've come to realize the deep truth in my mother's words. Each of us is created by God in a unique and flawless way. The circumstances of our birth hold no significance. It does not matter if we're born into nobility or humility. We should never underestimate ourselves or believe that someone else is superior. YOU ARE THE BEST!

Since the beginning of time, there has never been another person exactly like you. Your appearance, voice, laughter, and way of doing things are one-of-a-kind. Even among the 7.8 billion people on Earth, God knows you personally and completely. He even knows the number of hairs on your head (Luke 12:7). You are exceptional. You are God's masterpiece. Embrace this truth. Remind yourself every day, and you will see a spirit of confidence and excellence arise within you.

REFLECTION

CHAPTER 13
CHOOSING OUR BATTLES WISELY

"If it be possible, as much as lieth in you,
live peaceably with all men."
Romans 12:18

In life, we often face conflicts and challenges that test us. Some battles are worth fighting, while others are best left behind. As believers, we find comfort and guidance in seeking God's wisdom to discern when to stand up and when to take a different path.

When Jesus came into the world, angels were sent to protect Him. He had a vast battalion of angels at His disposal for His defense (Matthew 26:53). However, Jesus displayed incredible discernment in choosing when to fight and when to step back. For instance, as a baby, an angel directed Joseph in a dream to flee to Egypt with Jesus and Mary to escape Herod's harmful plans (Matthew 2:13). Despite having divine protection, Jesus took the path of flight as guided by God.

During His ministry, Jesus faced hostility in His hometown of Nazareth, where the crowd tried to harm Him (Luke 4:28-30). Despite His angelic protection, Jesus chose not to engage in physical conflict but walked away, illustrating the wisdom of following God's guidance.

History teaches us valuable lessons about unnecessary battles. King Josiah's decision to fight against King Necho of Egypt, despite God's warning, led to tragic consequences (2 Chronicles 35:20-23). From this account, we learn that many daily battles, such as disputes with neighbors, colleagues, or family members, are often inconsequential and avoidable. Sacrificing our well-being, whether figuratively or literally, for these trivial conflicts is not worth it.

As believers, we are called to live in peace with all people to the best of our ability (Romans 12:18). This verse encourages us to pursue harmony and unity, maintaining healthy relationships and avoiding unnecessary conflicts. By seeking God's wisdom through prayer and studying His Word, we can make better choices about the battles we engage in. Stepping away from a situation is not an act of cowardice but a display of the wisdom and discernment bestowed upon us by God.

In a world filled with conflicts and challenges, seeking God's wisdom in choosing our battles is essential. Jesus exemplified this discernment by knowing when to fight and when to retreat. Therefore, let us not allow trivial matters to drain our energy and jeopardize our well-being. Instead, may we seek peace, understanding, and resolution in the conflicts we encounter, relying on God's wisdom to guide us in making the right choices.

REFLECTION

CHAPTER 14
YOU ARE SPECIAL TO GOD

"But ye are a chosen generation, a royal priesthood, an holy nation, a peculiar people; that ye should shew forth the praises of him who hath called you out of darkness into his marvellous light:"
1 Peter 2:9

In a world that often tries to bring us down and make us feel small, it's important to understand how valuable and cherished we are in the eyes of our Heavenly Father.

Throughout the Bible, God speaks words of love and affection to His people. In 1 Peter 2:9, we are described as a chosen generation, a royal priesthood, a holy nation, and a peculiar people. God intentionally sets us apart, making us truly special. Being chosen means we're not just one among many; God personally called each of us, demonstrating His deep investment in our lives.

Think about the words God spoke about Jesus: "This is my beloved Son, in whom I am well pleased." At that time, Jesus was the only child of God, showing the incredible depth of God's love for

Him. Through Jesus' sacrifice, His death, burial, and resurrection, we have been adopted into God's family (Ephesians 1:4-5). We are now part of the family of God, with Jesus as our older brother. The same words of endearment spoken about Jesus now apply to us. We, too, are God's beloved sons and daughters.

Understanding that God's love for us is not based on our actions or accomplishments is crucial. His love is unconditional. Just like a mother's love for her child is not dependent on what the child does but on the child's existence, God's love for us is unwavering and constant. There's nothing that can make God stop loving us. No mistake, failure, or shortcoming can ever diminish His deep affection for us.

So, today, I encourage you to remember that you are special to God. You are not defined by your successes or failures but by the fact that you exist and are uniquely created by Him. Embrace your individuality and let God's love ignite your confidence as you walk in your divine purpose. Trust in His unwavering and everlasting love because you are treasured beyond measure.

REFLECTION

CHAPTER 15
DISCOVERING YOUR TRUE IDENTITY

"But now thus saith the LORD that created thee, O Jacob, and he that formed thee, O Israel, Fear not: for I have redeemed thee, I have called thee by thy name; thou art mine."
Isaiah 43:1

Have you ever thought about the question, "What's My Name?" It goes beyond the name given to us by our parents; it holds a deeper meaning and purpose. In the times of the Bible, names carried special significance, and people were often given new names to represent their divine destiny.

For example, in the scriptures, Abram became Abraham, symbolizing his role as the father of many nations. Jacob became Israel, marking his victory in wrestling with God and his new identity as the father of a nation.

Our name encompasses more than just a label. It reflects our character, personality, and unique qualities. It defines our position in life and encompasses our gifts, talents, and resources. When God calls us, He sees beyond society's labels, limitations, and external circumstances. He recognizes who He created us to be and the potential He placed within us. His calling is based on His divine perspective, our destined purpose, and the blessings He has given us.

Consider the example of Gideon, a young farmer who was called a "Mighty Warrior" by the angel of the Lord. Initially, Gideon felt unworthy and inadequate, questioning the name given to him. However, as he embraced his God-given name, he experienced remarkable victory and fulfilled his purpose.

God's call goes beyond our current circumstances and challenges. He may call us to roles or positions we never imagined possible. You may have no business experience, but the Spirit of God calls you an "International Businesswoman" or an "International Businessman." You may not have witnessed tangible miracles in your ministry, but God calls you a "Miracle Man or Woman." You may not have become a parent yet, but God calls you the "Mother of Kings." Embrace the name that God has given you.

Our response to His call unlocks our potential and propels us toward becoming who He designed us to be. When we say "Yes" to God's call, He promises to be with us on our journey. He will lead and guide us, directing us to the right places and connecting us with the right people. Our ability to become who we are meant to be is found in our response to God's call. As we say "Yes" to God, situations and circumstances will align, allowing us to step into our true identity.

As you ponder the question, "What's My Name?" remember that it explores a deeper realm of identity and purpose. Your name holds prophetic significance and reflects who God has called you to be. Embrace your God-given name, even if it seems different from your current reality. As you respond to God's call, He will navigate your journey, opening doors and orchestrating circumstances to fulfill His purpose in your life. Trust in His guidance, for your destiny awaits as you step into your true identity.

REFLECTION

CHAPTER 16
THE FRAGRANCE OF DIVINE FAVOR

"Now thanks be unto God, which always causeth us to triumph in Christ, and maketh manifest the savour of his knowledge by us in every place."
2 Corinthians 2:14

Have you ever thought about the impact your life has on others in the spiritual realm? As believers, we emit a captivating fragrance that draws favor and blessings. It's like a pleasant cologne or perfume that catches people's attention and creates a positive atmosphere.

According to 2 Corinthians 2:14, we carry a unique fragrance wherever we go. It's the fragrance of God's knowledge, a divine favor that manifests without any specific cause. This fragrance attracts help and blessings from others willingly.

When we are born again, this fragrance becomes a part of who we are. People are naturally drawn to the wisdom and revelation that flow from our lives. They see something special in us that they can't fully explain, and it opens doors, brings opportunities, and invites favor wherever we go.

Just as people are attracted to pleasant aromas, the fragrance of Christ within us acts as a magnet for others. We are not ordinary people in a crowd; we are divinely blessed and favored. Our lives testify to the greatness and victorious power of Christ.

It's important to recognize that we carry the fragrance of God's knowledge, a sweet aroma that attracts blessings and favor. With this understanding, we can confidently embrace our identity as beloved children of God. We can face each day with unwavering confidence, knowing that He always causes us to triumph. We can rejoice in Christ's victory and let the world see the greatness of our God through our lives (1 Corinthians 15:57).

As you move forward from this moment, remember the divine fragrance you carry. You have been marked by the sweet aroma of God's knowledge, drawing favor and blessings wherever you go. Embrace your identity as a cherished child of God and walk fearlessly in the triumph that Christ has secured for you.

REFLECTION

CHAPTER 17
THE ASSURANCE OF VICTORY

"What shall we then say to these things? If God be for us, who can be against us?"
Romans 8:31

Today, I want to encourage you with the powerful truth that in Christ, we always triumph. It's not just a possibility or an occasional outcome, but a promise that we can hold on to and declare over our lives.

Life's journey includes battles that test our faith and perseverance. It's important to distinguish between a battle and a war. Battles are individual rounds within the larger fight. Like in a boxing match, we may lose a round but still emerge victorious in the end.

As children of God, we are called to have a mindset of triumph. Even when we face setbacks in specific battles, we must never lose sight of the ultimate victory we have in Christ. When someone opposes us, we can ask ourselves, "Is God with me?" And if the answer is a resounding yes, then we can be assured of our triumph.

Romans 8:31 reminds us that if God is for us, no one can stand against us. So, take heart, God is on your side.

In 2 Corinthians 2:14, it says, "Thanks be to God, who always leads us as captives in Christ's triumphal procession." It's important to choose our battles wisely and avoid unnecessary conflicts. But no matter the challenges we face, we can rest assured that as children of God, we are destined to triumph. We have the firm assurance of victory in Christ. Let's embrace this truth and confidently declare it over our lives.

Walk forward with unwavering faith, knowing that your triumph is secure in Christ. Trust in His promises and let the assurance of victory propel you through every battle you face.

REFLECTION

CHAPTER 18
THE DANGER OF EXALTING OURSELVES

"For whosoever exalteth himself shall be abased; and he that humbleth himself shall be exalted."
Luke 14:11

The Bible teaches us an important lesson about humility using verses like Romans 12:3, Philippians 2:3-4, Proverbs 16:18, Luke 14:11, and James 4:6. These passages tell us to avoid thinking we're better or more important than others. Instead, God wants us to have a balanced view, understanding that our true worth comes from our relationship with Him, not our achievements or social status.

Sometimes we struggle with pride and want recognition and admiration from others. But the Bible reminds us that all honor and glory belong to God alone. He created us and provided everything we have. Taking credit for ourselves can harm our relationship with God and distort how we see ourselves and others.

Being humble does not mean putting ourselves down; it means accepting who we are based on what God says about us. It means seeing things from God's perspective instead of relying only on our own understanding. When we humble ourselves before God and accept His truths, we realize the incredible riches we have in Him. Even when we're going through tough times, God helps and lifts up those who are humble (Job 22:29).

To cultivate humility, we need to regularly check our thoughts, attitudes, and actions. When we notice pride creeping in, it's important to pause and change our thinking. Humility means putting others' needs first and serving them with love and kindness, just like Jesus showed us.

It's crucial to remember that humility does not make us less important or valuable. On the contrary, it helps us recognize our worth as unique creations of God. We should be grateful for the talents and blessings in our lives, acknowledging them as gifts from Him. When we choose humility, we align ourselves with God's plan, and He blesses us in amazing ways.

So, let's embrace the teachings of the Bible and fully embrace humility with joy and anticipation. Through humility, we show love for others, grow more like Jesus, and experience God's goodness in our lives.

REFLECTION

CHAPTER 19
DECLARED NOT GUILTY

"Therefore, being justified by faith, we have peace with God through our Lord Jesus Christ."
Romans 5:1

Today, I want to talk to you about the incredible power of forgiveness and freedom that comes from Jesus Christ. In 1 John 3:8-12, we learn that God sent His Son to destroy the devil's works. Understanding this truth can bring about a profound transformation in your life.

The devil often tries to remind us of our past mistakes, hoping to trap us in despair and bondage. However, 1 John 1:7-9 encourages us to walk in the light, openly admitting our sins, confessing them to God, and receiving His faithful forgiveness and cleansing. By doing this, we resist the enemy's tactics and fully embrace the freedom found in Christ.

Proverbs 10:12 teaches us the wisdom of love covering sins, while hatred stirs up strife. God, in His immense love for us, does not expose our deepest secrets or accuse us of past behaviors. Instead, He wants to help us overcome sin and live according to His Word.

Romans 5:1-2 reminds us that through faith, we are justified and find peace with God through Jesus Christ. We stand confidently in His grace, rejoicing in the hope of a glorious future in God's presence. In Christ, we are not only declared innocent but also cleansed by His precious blood.

Embracing forgiveness and freedom in Christ empowers us to live victorious lives, breaking free from guilt and shame. Remember, you have the strength to overcome, and God is with you every step of the way!

REFLECTION

CHAPTER 20
ENJOYING THE BLESSINGS OF THE COVENANT

"Wherefore, holy brethren, partakers of the heavenly calling, consider the Apostle and High Priest of our profession, Christ Jesus."
Hebrews 3:1

Accepting Jesus Christ as our Savior brings about an incredible transformation in our lives. His grace invites us to experience abundant blessings as we wholeheartedly follow Him and live according to His teachings.

In 1 Corinthians 15:10, the Apostle Paul humbly recognizes that his transformation and fruitful work for the Lord were not because of his own strength or abilities, but because of the magnificent grace of God working in him. We must also acknowledge that it is solely by God's grace that we are who we are today. When we invite Jesus into our hearts, His grace empowers us to live lives that bring glory to Him.

When we accept Jesus, His light shines on our path, guiding us even in dark times. Psalm 112:4 assures us that light arises for those who walk uprightly, even in challenging circumstances. We are never alone on this journey. God's grace, compassion, and righteousness are always with us as constant companions. By walking in His presence, we navigate life's trials with unwavering confidence, knowing that His guidance and love will sustain us.

As we align every aspect of our lives with God's eternal truth and principles, a profound transformation takes place within us. We are called to be holy and set apart for divine purposes. Hebrews 3:1 reminds us that we are holy brethren, chosen to participate in the heavenly calling. 1 Peter 2:9 reinforces our identity as a chosen generation, a royal priesthood, and a holy nation. Embracing these truths, we gradually transform our thoughts, actions, and character. The Holy Spirit actively works in us, shaping us to become more like Christ, from glory to even greater glory.

Friends, embracing Jesus Christ as our Lord and Savior opens the door to profound blessings. Through His grace, we experience a remarkable transformation and are empowered to live lives that honor and glorify God. Let us embark on this beautiful journey with hope in our hearts, embracing the abundant blessings of the covenant.

REFLECTION

CHAPTER 21
THE REWARDS OF GIVING JESUS YOUR BOAT

"And they that be wise shall shine as the brightness of the firmament; and they that turn many to righteousness as the stars for ever and ever."
Daniel 12:3

Did you know that you have a boat? Yes, you do. Today, I want to talk to you about it. In this modern age, we are fortunate to have amazing tools like social media that help us connect with people from all walks of life. As followers of Jesus, we have a special opportunity to use these platforms to share His love and message with a wide audience.

The story of Simon Peter in Luke 5:1-8 beautifully illustrates the blessings that come when we entrust our boat, our platform, and our lives to Jesus. After teaching, Jesus tells Simon Peter to go out into the deep and cast his nets for a catch. Simon, a seasoned fisherman, doubts because they had been fishing all night and caught nothing.

But despite his weariness, Simon says, "Nevertheless, at Your word, I will let down the net." His faith in Jesus compels him to obey.

As Simon Peter casts the net, something incredible happens. They catch so many fish that their nets start to break, and they signal their partners in the other boat for help. Both boats become filled with fish, to the point of almost sinking. It's an amazing display of God's provision!

This powerful story shows that Jesus is the true light who brings rewards to everyone. When we give Jesus our boat, our platform, our lives, He blesses us abundantly. Just as Simon Peter received an overflowing catch of fish, Jesus rewards us when we step out in faith and trust Him. He honors our obedience and commitment.

Remember, Jesus is the ultimate reward. When we surrender our boats to Him, He brings blessings beyond our expectations. So, let's use our social media platforms as boats to uplift, encourage, and inspire others. Let's share our stories of encountering Jesus and the impact He has had on our lives. There are incredible blessings when you entrust your boat to Jesus!

REFLECTION

CHAPTER 22
HAVING SOMETHING TO MULTIPLY

---

*"For ye know the grace of our Lord Jesus Christ, that,
though he was rich, yet for your sakes he became poor,
that ye through his poverty might be rich."*
2 Corinthians 8:9

The Bible consistently speaks of abundance in our lives. In 2 Corinthians 8:9, we are reminded of the grace of Jesus Christ, who, despite His wealth, chose to become poor so that through His poverty, we could experience richness. However, it's important to understand our role in this process. We are called to contribute.

In 2 Kings 4:1-4, we meet a widow facing a dire situation. Overwhelmed by debt and the potential enslavement of her sons, she sought help from the prophet Elisha. When asked about her possessions, she sadly replied, "Your servant has nothing in the house except a jar of oil."

Elisha's response to her distressing situation was surprising and enlightening. He told her to gather empty vessels and pour her small supply of oil into them. Astonishingly, that small jar of oil multiplied until every vessel she had collected was filled. Miraculously, she not only paid off her debts but also had enough to sustain her family.

This story teaches us an important lesson: to experience multiplication, we need to have something to offer. While this principle extends beyond material possessions, it highlights the importance of diligence and resourcefulness. God does not bless idleness; instead, He calls us to work diligently and be proactive in pursuing our goals.

Proverbs 10:4-5 consistently reminds us that diligence leads to abundance, while laziness can result in poverty. Diligence encompasses all aspects of our lives, extending beyond financial well-being. It encourages us to be proactive in our relationships, careers, and spiritual growth. When we give our best in every endeavor, we acknowledge that God rewards our efforts.

Proverbs 13:22 emphasizes the legacy of a good person who leaves an inheritance for future generations. Approaching life with diligence, integrity, compassion, and a desire to make a positive impact positions us to receive God's blessings. While wealth obtained through sinful means may be temporary, the righteous inherit everlasting riches.

God desires to multiply what we bring to the table, but it starts with our diligence and resourcefulness. Let's remain proactive in pursuing our goals, diligent in our work, and faithful in our service to God and others. May we experience blessings and multiplication in every area of our lives. Amen!

REFLECTION

CHAPTER 23
THE VICTORIOUS PATH OF FAITH

"...Thus, saith the LORD unto you, Be not afraid nor dismayed by reason of this great multitude; for the battle is not yours, but God's."
2 Chronicles 20:15

I want to remind you never to give up, no matter the challenges you face. Our faith is in a powerful God who can do the impossible. In our Kingdom, victory is certain for those who have faith and fight the good fight.

Our journey of faith requires determination, resilience, and unwavering belief in God's promises. The battles we face are not just physical but spiritual, against forces that try to hold us back. In these moments, we must stand strong, holding onto our faith and embracing the eternal life we've been called to.

Our God is not limited by barriers or obstacles. He can make a way where there seems to be none, just as He did for the Israelites at the Red Sea. When we face impossible situations, we can trust that God will provide a path for us. True defeat only happens if we give up. But thanks to God, our faith ensures that we are more than conquerors, no matter the circumstances.

On our journey, we will encounter bad news and discouragement. But we must not let them crush us. Instead, let them fuel our determination to seek God's wisdom and find new strategies. Bad news can become opportunities for growth and steppingstones to greater victories.

Brothers and sisters, always remember that faith is the key to overcoming life's obstacles. Trust in the God who can do the impossible. Hold onto the call to fight the good fight, knowing that victory is guaranteed in our Kingdom.

REFLECTION

CHAPTER 24
STRIVING FOR CONTENTMENT

"But godliness with contentment is great gain."
1 Timothy 6:6

In today's world, driven by social media and the constant pursuit of more, finding contentment can be challenging, especially when it comes to our relationship with money and possessions. The book of Hebrews offers valuable insights, warning against excessive love for money and urging us to resist greed while maintaining a balanced perspective.

Throughout history, we've seen people like Judas Iscariot who prioritized personal gain above all else, even betraying others. Such individuals often avoid hard work and commitment. It's important to remember that God does not favor idleness; Proverbs 16:27 reminds us that idle hands are the devil's workshop.

As followers of Jesus, we are called to cultivate a spirit of contentment in our hearts. Mammon, which represents the pursuit of money and material possessions, often tempts us to constantly want more. But true contentment is not found in getting wealth; it is found in our relationship with God.

The apostle Paul sets an example for us in the Bible when he says in Philippians 4:11-13 that he has learned to be content in all situations, whether he has a lot or a little. Paul's contentment comes from his deep faith in God's provision and control over his life. We are also encouraged to find joy and satisfaction in God's presence, knowing He knows our needs and will take care of us.

Being content frees us from the constant desire to compare ourselves with others or always want more. It brings peace to our hearts, knowing we have chosen what is truly important — a life centered on God's love, grace, and eternal promises.

So, let us strive to be content in all situations, find joy in God's presence, and trust in His provision. In doing so, we will experience a richness that goes beyond the allure of money, and we will walk in the abundance of God's blessings and the fulfillment of His purpose for our lives.

REFLECTION

CHAPTER 25
LIBERATION THROUGH THE TRUTH

"Therefore, if any man be in Christ, he is a new creature: old things are passed away; behold, all things are become new."
2 Corinthians 5:17

In a world where judgment and condemnation are common, it's comforting to know that our past mistakes don't define our relationship with God. According to 2 Corinthians 5:17, when we accept Christ, we become new creations. Our past sins no longer determine who we are; we are made new in Him. God's endless grace washes away our wrongdoings, giving us a fresh start and pouring His love and mercy upon our lives.

The heart of our faith is the powerful ministry of reconciliation. In 2 Corinthians 5:18-19, Paul explains that God, through Jesus Christ, brings us back into a harmonious relationship with Himself. In this incredible act of love, God does not hold our sins against us. Instead, He forgives us entirely and forgets our wrongdoings, removing them as far as the East is from the West. This extraordinary exchange was made possible by Jesus, who willingly carried our sins on the cross, bridging the gap between us and God.

Knowing that God does not keep a record of our sins brings true freedom. As new creations, we are empowered to live righteously, no longer controlled by the power of sin. Even though we still face temptations and challenges, we can be confident that God's forgiveness and transforming power help us overcome them. We can embrace a life marked by righteousness, guided by His grace and the presence of His Spirit within us.

REFLECTION

CHAPTER 26
FORGIVENESS IS A CHOICE

"And be ye kind one to another, tenderhearted, forgiving one another, even as God for Christ's sake hath forgiven you."
Ephesians 4:32

When conflicts arise, it can be challenging to forgive and find resolution. But as followers of Christ, we are called to embody His teachings of love, forgiveness, and reconciliation.

In Luke 17:3-5, we learn how to handle conflicts within the Christian community. It tells us to address wrongdoing and offer forgiveness when someone truly repents. Even if they hurt us repeatedly, we should still forgive them if they sincerely apologize. This requires having a forgiving mindset and showing grace, even in challenging situations.

Forgiveness is a powerful tool for healing and restoration when we're hurt. It's a choice based on our faith and understanding of God's love. By realizing that God can turn difficult situations for good, like the story of Joseph in Genesis 50:20-21, we can let go of our pain and trust in His greater plan. Joseph's brothers, driven by jealousy, had sold him into slavery. Years later, Joseph, now a powerful ruler in Egypt, had the opportunity to seek revenge when his brothers came seeking food during a famine. However, Joseph chose to forgive them, acknowledging that God had a purpose in their actions. Joseph's act of forgiveness is a powerful example of how forgiveness can bring healing and restoration to broken relationships.

Another example of forgiveness in the Bible can be found in the story of Jesus Christ. When Jesus was being crucified, He said, "Father, forgive them, for they don't know what they are doing" (Luke 23:34). Despite being wrongly accused and suffering greatly, Jesus chose to forgive those who were crucifying Him, including the Roman soldiers and the religious leaders who had planned His arrest and trial.

Jesus' act of forgiveness shows His teachings on love and forgiveness in action. It demonstrates His ability to offer forgiveness even in the midst of great injustice and pain. Through His forgiveness, Jesus sets an extraordinary example of grace and mercy, revealing that forgiveness has the power to bring about redemption and reconciliation.

Jesus' act of forgiveness teaches us an important lesson. Despite facing injustice and suffering, He chose to forgive. This shows us the value of adopting a mindset focused on forgiveness and reconciliation. As followers of Christ, we should approach conflicts with humility, communicate openly, and seek resolution through forgiveness. By embracing forgiveness, we can find healing, personal growth, and reflect God's love and mercy to others. Let's learn from Jesus' example and become agents of reconciliation, bringing God's healing grace to a world in need.

REFLECTION

CHAPTER 27
LIVING WITH DIPLOMATIC IMMUNITY

"They are not of the world, even as I am not of the world."
John 17:16

It is comforting to know that, as believers, we are kept by God while still in this world. We may physically reside in a particular country or community, but we are not bound by the negative influences and principalities that rule over them. Hallelujah! In fact, we can live right here on Earth with diplomatic immunity, governed by a higher power and guided by a different set of principles.

In John 17:11-15, Jesus prayed to the Father, acknowledging that He would leave the world, but His disciples would remain. He asked the Father to keep them in His name, uniting them as He and the Father are one. While Jesus was physically present, He safeguarded His disciples in the name of the Father, ensuring their safety, except for the one who was meant for destruction as prophesied. Jesus spoke these words to give His disciples joy as He prepared to return to the Father.

Jesus also acknowledged that the world would hate His disciples because they were not part of it, just as He wasn't. Despite the opposition and hatred, Jesus didn't pray for His disciples to be taken out of the world, but rather, He prayed for them to be protected from evil. This prayer shows that we, as followers of Christ, are not exempt from the challenges and trials of this world. However, we find comfort in knowing that God is our shield, guarding us from the surrounding evil.

To live with this diplomatic immunity, it's essential to have a mindset of the just. Having a mindset of the just means aligning our thoughts, actions, and attitudes with the standards set by God. It involves standing firm in truth and integrity, refusing to compromise our values for temporary worldly gain. This mindset allows us to navigate through the complexities of the world while remaining true to our beliefs.

My friends, striving to develop and nurture this mindset not only brings honor and glory to God but also allows us to live our lives with diplomatic immunity and experience the freedom that comes with divine protection.

REFLECTION

CHAPTER 28
SEEKING A SIGN

"Ask thee a sign of the LORD thy God; ask it either in the depth, or in the height above."
Isaiah 7:11

God's love for us is boundless, and He has given us the precious gift of free will. This gift allows us to make important choices that shape our lives, such as who to marry, where to live, and what career path to follow. However, we must cautiously approach these decisions, seek God's guidance, patiently wait for His perfect timing, and ask for signs when unsure. A sign? Yes, asking for a sign from God is not a lack of faith but rather a humble expression of our desire to align our will with His.

In Isaiah 7:10-15, we encounter Ahaz during a challenging time. God, in His faithfulness, instructed Ahaz to ask for a sign as confirmation of His guidance. Unfortunately, Ahaz hesitated, fearing that requesting a sign would test God's faithfulness. Nevertheless, even in the face of Ahaz's doubt, God graciously provided a sign—the prophecy of the virgin birth of Immanuel. This story teaches us that seeking a sign from God is not a lack of faith, but rather a humble act of seeking His guidance and confirmation.

The story of Gideon in Judges 6-7 beautifully illustrates the importance of seeking God's guidance and patiently waiting for His timing. Gideon faced overwhelming odds as he prepared to confront the Midianites. Filled with uncertainty, Gideon sought reassurance from God, requesting a sign that would strengthen his resolve. In His loving mercy, God granted Gideon's request by orchestrating a dream and its interpretation, assuring Gideon of His enduring presence, and empowering him to overcome. This account reminds us that asking for a sign in times of uncertainty can lead to clarity and assurance in our decision-making process.

In today's fast-paced society, there is a strong temptation to rush into decisions without considering God's timing or seeking His guidance. However, the stories of Ahaz and Gideon offer valuable wisdom about the importance of patience and asking for signs from God. Let us avoid making hasty choices that may impact our lives and those around us. Instead, let us dedicate time to seek God's wisdom, ask for His guidance, and patiently wait for His confirmation. By doing so, we can confidently navigate life's decisions, knowing that we are aligning our will with His and allowing His perfect plan to unfold in our lives.

REFLECTION

CHAPTER 29
BOASTING IN THE LORD

"But he that glorieth, let him glory in the Lord."
2 Corinthians 10:17

In our journey to live an authentic Christian life, it is important to take time for self-reflection and evaluate our priorities and spirituality based on biblical principles. Instead of being overly focused on material possessions or having a prideful attitude, our focus should be on cultivating a deep and meaningful relationship with God and embracing the presence of Jesus in our lives.

The Scriptures remind us that boasting about ourselves, or our accomplishments is unproductive and displeasing to God. Instead, we are encouraged to find our worth and completeness in Him alone (1 Corinthians 1:31, 2 Corinthians 10:17). When we become consumed with self-importance, we hinder the work of the Holy Spirit, who desires to work through those who are humble. Therefore, let us humbly seek to honor the Lord in all that we do.

Our spirituality is not measured by what we own on Earth, but by how much we reflect the character of Jesus. Jesus teaches us seek the Kingdom of God above all else and live righteously, and He will give us everything we need. (Matthew 6:33). The cars, houses, and other material possessions should not be the standard by which we evaluate our spiritual growth. Instead, we should focus on nurturing a deep relationship with Jesus Christ and allowing His love and teachings to shape our lives.

It is important to clarify that being a Christian does not mean we must be destitute. Contrary to common misconceptions, there is nothing inherently wrong with wealth. In the kingdom of God, money can be a resource to advance His purposes and bless others. However, the danger lies in becoming arrogant and placing our trust solely in uncertain riches (1 Timothy 6:17). Our trust should be firmly rooted in the living God, who graciously provides us with everything to enjoy. By adopting a generous and humble attitude towards wealth, we can use it wisely for God's glory and the well-being of others.

REFLECTION

CHAPTER 30
THE HEART OF WORSHIP

"But the hour cometh, and now is, when the true worshippers shall worship the Father in spirit and in truth: for the Father seeketh such to worship him."
John 4:23

Worship is a beautiful act of humility before God, where we express our gratitude and reflect on His goodness. It connects us intimately with God, allowing us to show our deep reverence and devotion to the One who deserves all praise.

In the past, people used to worship by following rituals and making offerings to honor God, but Jesus taught us that true worship goes beyond outward actions.

In a conversation with a Samaritan woman, Jesus explained that true worship happens when we approach God with sincerity and truth (John 4:23). When we genuinely worship God, we focus on Him and express our love, creating a space for Him to show Himself to us. It means aligning our hearts and minds with His character and trying to honor Him in everything we do. Worship is not limited to specific times or places; it's an ongoing attitude of surrender and gratitude. When we do this, we foster a closer relationship with our Creator, who wants to know us personally as His children.

Offering is also an important part of worship. Proverbs 3:9-10 reminds us to honor the Lord with our possessions and first fruits. When we willingly and joyfully give our resources, talents, and time, we demonstrate our trust in God's provision and acknowledge His sovereignty over our lives. As we offer ourselves as living sacrifices, our worship goes beyond words, becoming a tangible expression of love and gratitude.

Worship also recognizes that all blessings come from God. In His presence, we find complete joy and everlasting pleasures (Psalm 16:11). Approaching Him with a grateful heart, acknowledging His goodness and faithfulness, cultivates an atmosphere of worship. It opens our eyes to the countless blessings bestowed upon us and helps us fully appreciate the richness of His grace.

Honoring those whom God has appointed as spiritual leaders is another aspect of worship. Galatians 6:6-8 encourages us to support and bless those who teach and guide us in God's ways. By investing in their lives, we actively participate in the work of the kingdom and experience the abundant harvest that comes from sowing seeds of obedience and generosity.

As we worship in spirit and truth, we deepen our connection with God, allowing our thoughts, words, and actions to reflect genuine love and profound reverence for the Almighty.

REFLECTION

CHAPTER 31
SUBMITTING TO HIS WILL

"For I know the thoughts that I think toward you, saith the LORD, thoughts of peace, and not of evil, to give you an expected end."
Jeremiah 29:11

We often face trials, challenges, and temptations that try to steer us away from God's path for our lives. The devil, our adversary, constantly seeks to deceive and lead us astray. To discern between the devil's schemes and God's plans, we must humbly submit to our Heavenly Father's will.

When we surrender to God, we acknowledge His authority and wisdom, recognizing that He knows what is best for us beyond our understanding. In this surrender, we find true freedom and the assurance that God is in control.

As believers, we express our faith through declarations, speaking God's truth into our lives and circumstances. However, once we make these declarations, it's important to release them to God's capable hands, trusting that He hears our prayers and is actively working on our behalf. Letting go and entrusting our desires to His care allows Him to work in His perfect timing and wisdom.

In our prayers, it's crucial to include the phrase, "Let your perfect will be done." By doing so, we acknowledge that God's will surpasses our own desires. We understand that He knows what is ultimately best for us, even if it does not align with our immediate expectations. Aligning our prayers with God's perfect will demonstrates our trust in His wisdom and invites Him to guide our steps on the right path.

In the Gospel of Mark, Jesus shares a parable about the kingdom of God using the analogy of a man sowing seeds. The growth of the seeds is a gradual and mysterious process. Similarly, God's plans for our lives may not always be immediately evident or clear to us. There may be seasons of uncertainty or difficulty, but we can take comfort in knowing that the harvest is coming. God's faithfulness will bear fruit in due time.

In the book of Jeremiah, God assures us of His plans, saying, "For I know the plans I have for you, declares the Lord, plans for welfare and not for evil, to give you a future and a hope" (Jeremiah 29:11). Even in unfavorable circumstances, we can find hope and assurance knowing that God has a purpose and a bright future for each of us.

Though trials may come our way, and they will, we know that greatness awaits us in the future. In times of need, we can find solace in the presence of the Holy Spirit —our Comforter, Counselor, Encourager, and Helper.

REFLECTION

CHAPTER 32
THE DYNAMIC TRIO

"And now abideth faith, hope, charity, these three; but the greatest of these is charity."
1 Corinthians 13:13

I want to take a moment to remind you of the incredible significance of faith, hope, and love in our lives. These three virtues are like pillars that support our faith and enrich our relationships with God and others.

First, let's talk about hope. It's more than wishful thinking or fleeting optimism. It's a powerful force that comes from our unwavering belief in God's promises. The apostle Paul reminds us in his letter to the Romans that the God of hope fills us with joy and peace as we trust in Him. Through the Holy Spirit, our hope grows, sustains us during difficult times, and inspires us to keep moving forward. Hope anchors our souls, reminding us that God's goodness will prevail, and His promises will be fulfilled.

Next is faith. It is the channel through which we receive God's abundant blessings. Jesus Himself emphasized the importance of unwavering faith in God because it opens the door to supernatural possibilities. When we have genuine faith, believe in our hearts, and speak with conviction, we witness God's remarkable power at work. We experience God's grace through faith and see His promises come to life in extraordinary ways.

Finally, we come to love—the greatest of them all. Love finds its highest expression in God's profound and unconditional love for humanity. As John 3:16 tells us, God loved us so much that He gave His only Son, Jesus Christ, so that we may have eternal life through Him. Love goes beyond selfish desires and embraces selflessness. It compels us to love others as Christ loved us, offering forgiveness, grace, and compassion. The love of Christ within us empowers us to live transformed lives, keeping us from worldly passions and guiding us to align our actions with God's will. It reflects our identification with Christ's crucifixion and resurrection, as Paul firmly declares in 2 Corinthians 5:14.

Thanks be to God for weaving hope, faith, and love together to form the fabric of our Christian existence. As believers, we hold firmly to the hope found in God's promises, trusting in His faithfulness to fulfill His Word. Through genuine faith, we position ourselves to receive God's blessings and breakthroughs. Fueled by the boundless love of Christ, we become vessels overflowing with His love, sharing it generously with a world in need. As we develop these virtues in our lives, we not only bring hope to others but also become recipients of God's abundant blessings.

REFLECTION

CHAPTER 33
PRAYING FOR GOD'S SENT LEADERS

"Finally, brethren, pray for us, that the word of the Lord may have free course, and be glorified, even as it is with you."
2 Thessalonians 3:1

In the spiritual realm, an ongoing battle exists between the forces of light and darkness. The adversary tirelessly seeks to attack and undermine the men and women of God who have been called to lead and guide His people. However, we have been bestowed with a powerful weapon: prayer. Through intercession for those anointed by God, we can provide a shield of spiritual protection against the schemes of the enemy.

Just as Jesus warned His disciples in Matthew 26:31 about their impending offense, the enemy still seeks to attack men and women of God who have been called to minister. Nevertheless, our prayers possess extraordinary power to disrupt the plans of the enemy.

When we intercede on behalf of these individuals, we stand in the gap, providing them with a covering of spiritual protection.

The Lord faithfully defends and safeguards those whom He has called and anointed to lead His people. In Psalm 89:19-23, we learn about David, whom God chose and blessed. The psalmist assures us that God helped and strengthened David, ensuring that his enemies couldn't overcome him. Similarly, when we fervently pray for God's chosen ones, we align ourselves with His divine protection, and He fights for them.

As believers, we have a responsibility to pray for the leaders whom God has sent to edify and guide us. The apostle Paul, in 1 Thessalonians 5:25 and 2 Thessalonians 3:1, explicitly requests brethrens to pray for him and his fellow workers. Likewise, we are called to intercede for those who minister the Word of God to us. Our prayers should focus on their spiritual discernment so that their eyes may be opened to perceive the truth, their ears attuned to the Holy Spirit's voice, and their minds enlightened to understand God's will. Through our prayers, we create space for the Holy Spirit to inspire their words and empower their ministry.

Let us remember the teachings of Jesus, who cautioned His disciples about the enemy's scheme to strike the shepherd and scatter the sheep. Through intercession, we align ourselves with God's divine purposes and actively contribute to the protection and empowerment of His anointed ones. Hallelujah! Our fervent, unwavering faith will counteract the enemy's plans and bring glory to His name.

REFLECTION

CHAPTER 34
STEADFAST IN PURPOSE

"Alas! for that day is great, so that none is like it: it is even the time of Jacob's trouble; but he shall be saved out of it."
Jeremiah 30:7

Trials are never something we desire, but our attitude during those moments can make all the difference. Today, let's find inspiration in the story of Joseph and Potiphar's wife and see how Joseph's unwavering commitment to his purpose propelled him to prominence in Egypt.

Potiphar's wife was a significant distraction in Joseph's life. She persistently tried to seduce him, but he remained faithful to God and committed to his responsibilities as a servant in Potiphar's household. Joseph understood that giving in to temptation would not only betray his master but also violate his relationship with God. Despite her relentless efforts and false accusations, Joseph held on to his integrity.

Joseph's ability to resist temptation and overcome distractions came from his unwavering devotion to God's purpose for his life. He knew that his journey was not about personal satisfaction but about fulfilling God's plan. By focusing on his divine calling, Joseph managed to rise above the challenges and setbacks he faced.

The Bible reminds us to be prepared for spiritual battles, even during peaceful times. Joseph's encounter with Potiphar's wife serves as a reminder that distractions and temptations can arise unexpectedly, even when everything seems fine. In times of tranquility, we must strengthen our spiritual foundation by deepening our relationship with God and equipping ourselves with His Word. This preparation empowers us to stand firm and resist the traps that try to derail us from our intended path.

Joseph's journey was far from easy. He experienced betrayal, false accusations, and imprisonment. Similarly, we must acknowledge that trials and challenges are part of our own journeys. The Bible even warns us about the time of Jacob's trouble in Jeremiah 30:7. Adversity can come in various forms, such as distractions, temptations, or even persecution. However, just as Joseph emerged victorious from his trials, we can also find strength and courage in God's promises, knowing that He remains faithful to deliver us. Our purpose is too important to be compromised by temporary pleasures or worldly distractions. Let's stay committed to God's calling, trusting in His strength and provision.

REFLECTION

CHAPTER 35
BECOMING PEOPLE AFTER GOD'S HEART

"But seek ye first the kingdom of God, and his righteousness; and all these things shall be added unto you."
Matthew 6:33

As believers in Christ, our main goal is to become people who reflect God's heart, just like David was described in 1 Samuel 13:14. But what does it mean to have a heart like God's, and how can we achieve it?

First and foremost, we should make God's kingdom and righteousness our top priority, as emphasized in Matthew 6:33. This means seeking His will and aligning our lives with His purposes. By placing God at the center of our lives, surrendering our own desires, and aligning our priorities with His, we position ourselves to experience His blessings and guidance in every area of life. When we prioritize God, we demonstrate our devotion and recognize Him as the ultimate source of all our needs.

Additionally, we can learn from the examples of those who have walked the path of faith before us. Take Solomon, the son of King David, who desired to continue his father's legacy by serving God wholeheartedly. In 1 Kings 3, Solomon approached God humbly, seeking wisdom to lead God's people well. His example teaches us the value of learning from spiritual leaders, mentors and the timeless wisdom found in Scripture. Drawing inspiration from their insights, we can enrich our journey, make wiser choices, and deepen our understanding of God's ways. Learning from others helps us build a strong foundation of knowledge and grow in wisdom.

Lastly, we must actively pursue wisdom and understanding. King David passed down his wisdom to Solomon, as seen in the book of Proverbs. In Proverbs 4, David emphasizes the importance of embracing wisdom and understanding. Pursuing wisdom is an ongoing journey that involves seeking knowledge, discernment, and insight. It requires humility, a teachable spirit, a willingness to learn from God's Word, and a commitment to applying its principles daily. As we deepen our understanding of God's truth and seek His guidance, we grow in wisdom and become better equipped to make choices that align with His heart.

As followers of Christ, our ultimate goal is to mirror God's heart. We can achieve this by making God's kingdom and righteousness our priority, learning from those who labored before us, and actively seeking wisdom and understanding. May we continually seek God's presence, align our lives with His purposes, and embark on a lifelong journey of growing in knowledge and imaging His heart to the world around us.

REFLECTION

CHAPTER 36
NURTURING A POSITIVE MINDSET

*"For as he thinketh in his heart, so is he: Eat and drink,
saith he to thee; but his heart is not with thee."*
Proverbs 23:7

The things we say and the thoughts we have greatly impact who we are and what we do. Proverbs 23:7 teaches us that our thoughts shape our character. Therefore, it's important to examine our thoughts and ensure that they align with God's truth and what truly matters. Understanding the power of our words and thoughts helps us realize the importance of speaking positively, resisting negativity, and filling our minds with God's Word.

In our healing and deliverance services, I often talk about how our words shape our lives. Our words have the power to change our circumstances, just like God created the world with His words. When we speak words of faith and declare God's promises, we can make a positive difference in our situation. For example, Exodus

15:26 tells us that God is our healer. Even if we don't feel well, we can trust in those words, speak them with faith, and focus on God's truth instead of negative thoughts that come from the enemy.

It's important to remember not to speak words that support the devil's actions. James 3:4 teaches us about the incredible power of our words. Just like a small rudder can steer a large ship, our tongues can shape our lives and have a significant impact on others. The devil always tries to make us doubt and be afraid by using lies and tricks. One of his tactics is to make us say things that reflect doubt, fear, and negativity. But as followers of Jesus, we should resist the temptation to speak the devil's lies. Instead, let's use our words to encourage and uplift ourselves and others. When we speak God's truth and declare His promises, we reject the devil's influence and create an atmosphere of faith and victory.

It's also crucial to change our way of thinking. We're not perfect, and God knows that. That's why He invites us to keep renewing our minds by focusing on what He says in His Word. Romans 12:2 tells us not to think and act like the world does, but to let God change the way we think. When we immerse ourselves in the Bible, we gain wisdom and understanding. This helps us see things from God's point of view. As we meditate on God's truth, it starts to change the way we think and empowers us to make decisions that are in line with His will. This renewed thinking helps us resist temptation, overcome challenges, and live wisely.

To sum it up, our words hold significant power. Therefore, it's essential to be mindful of what we say. Let's speak life and declare God's promises. This way, we can reject negativity and cultivate a positive and progressive environment.

REFLECTION

CHAPTER 37
FIGHTING THE GOOD FIGHT

"Fight the good fight of faith, lay hold on eternal life,
whereunto thou art also called, and hast professed a
good profession before many witnesses."
1 Timothy 6:12

The Bible encourages us to engage in a special kind of fight –
the good fight of faith. It's important to understand that this
fight is not against physical enemies or people, but against spiritual
forces and the darkness in our world. In 1 Timothy 6:12, the
apostle Paul reminds us to "Fight the good fight of faith, lay hold
on eternal life, whereunto thou art also called, and hast professed a
good profession before many witnesses."

But why is it called a good fight? The answer lies in the assurance
of victory. Hallelujah! When we enter this battle, we do so with
the knowledge that victory is already guaranteed through Christ.
Our triumph does not rely on our own strength or abilities, but on
the power and faithfulness of the Lord. In every battle we face, we
fight from a position of victory because Christ has already won the
ultimate battle on our behalf.

To fight this good fight effectively, we need to equip ourselves with the armor of God. In Ephesians 6:12-13, Paul vividly describes our struggle: "For we wrestle not against flesh and blood, but against principalities, against powers, against the rulers of the darkness of this world, against spiritual wickedness in high places. Wherefore take unto you the whole armor of God, that ye may be able to withstand in the evil day, and having done all, to stand."

The armor of the Spirit is not physical; it is composed of the truths and promises found in God's Word. Just as physical armor protects and defends a soldier in battle, the Word of God serves as our spiritual safeguard and shield. In Ephesians 6:17, the Bible refers to it as the "Sword of the Spirit." This powerful weapon equips us to withstand the ceaseless onslaught of the enemy, granting us strength, guidance, and discernment.

In the face of spiritual battles, we must immerse ourselves in the Scriptures, meditating on its truths and applying them to our lives. The Word of God strengthens our faith, enlightens our understanding, and empowers us to stand firm in adversity. It reveals God's character, His unfailing promises, and His perfect will for our lives. The more we know and internalize His Word, the better equipped we become to fight the good fight of faith.

Therefore, let us firmly hold on to the Word of God as our ultimate weapon and source of strength. Let us continually study and meditate on it, allowing it to renew our minds and guide our steps. By doing so, we will be fully prepared for our battles, knowing that victory is already secured in Christ. So, my fellow believers, let us courageously fight the good fight, for the Word of God is our unwavering anchor during life's storms.

REFLECTION

CHAPTER 38
PRAY FOR YOUR COUNTRY

"And seek the peace of the city whither I have caused you to be carried away captives and pray unto the LORD for it: for in the peace thereof shall ye have peace."
Jeremiah 29:7

In our fast-paced world, it's easy to overlook the importance of praying for our country, nation, president, and leaders. However, as Christians, we have a higher calling. We are called to pray for our leaders, regardless of our political views, and to intercede for our nation before God.

Praying for our leaders is not just a suggestion; it's a biblical command. In his letter to Timothy, the apostle Paul urged believers to offer supplications, prayers, intercessions, and thanksgiving for all people, including kings and those in authority (1 Timothy 2:1-2). This command applies to every season and every leader, underscoring the importance of seeking God's guidance for those who govern our country.

Jeremiah 29:7 reminds us to seek the peace and prosperity of the city we live in, and this applies to our role as citizens of a nation as well. We are called to pray for our country, seeking its well-being, because when our nation thrives, we also benefit. Our prayers have the power to influence the trajectory of our nation and the hearts of our leaders.

It's crucial to understand that our prayers for our country go beyond personal preferences or political ideologies. Our focus should be on seeking God's will, wisdom, and guidance for our leaders as they make decisions that impact our nation's welfare. We should pray for integrity, wisdom, and discernment to be bestowed upon our leaders, regardless of their political affiliations.

We should also pray for unity within our nation. During times of division and conflict, our prayers can help bridge gaps between different groups and foster an environment of understanding, respect, and reconciliation. As Christians, we are called to be peacemakers and agents of change, and our prayers play a vital role in that process.

Proverbs 21:1 reminds us that the king's heart is in the hands of the Lord, and He can turn it wherever He desires. Our prayers have the ability to touch the hearts of our leaders, soften them, and align them with God's purposes. We should never underestimate the impact our prayers can have on the decisions made by those in positions of authority.

Prayer is not a passive activity; it's a powerful weapon in the hands of believers. Through prayer, we tap into God's unlimited power and invite Him to work in our nation, leaders, and lives. As we pray, we humbly acknowledge our dependence on God and His sovereignty over everything. Let our prayers be filled with faith, humility, and love as we intercede for the peace, prosperity, and well-being of our land.

REFLECTION

CHAPTER 39
A STRONG TOWER

"The name of the LORD is a strong tower: the righteous runneth into it and is safe."
Proverbs 18:10

Every kingdom has a fortress that offers protection and security to its citizens. In the same way, the Bible teaches us that the name of the Lord is a strong tower—a place of safety and refuge. When we accept Jesus as our Savior, we become citizens of Zion, embraced within the loving arms of the heavenly city. This special citizenship sets us apart and gives us divine protection and abundant provision.

But what does this strong tower represent? Proverbs 18:10 tells us that the name of the Lord signifies unwavering strength, unyielding security, and impenetrable protection. When we genuinely call upon the name of Jesus, we access boundless power and unmatched authority. It's important to understand the deep significance of Jesus' name—it represents who He is, His character, and the saving grace He offers. No matter what challenges we face—whether physical, emotional, or spiritual—invoking the name of Jesus brings us into His divine presence, where we find comfort, shelter, and deliverance.

As believers, we receive a new citizenship—one that goes beyond the limitations of this earthly realm and connects us with the heavenly realm. Isaiah 33:20 depicts Zion, the city of our gatherings. As citizens of Zion, we are freed from the constraints and uncertainties of this world. In God's kingdom, we discover unmatched divine protection, abundant provision, and an unshakable peace that surpasses all understanding.

As citizens of Zion, we participate in God's divine nature, fully supported by the governance of heaven. Our victory does not depend on our own strength or abilities; it rests on God's unwavering faithfulness and indomitable power. By trusting in Him and relying on His strength, we go beyond being mere conquerors and emerge victorious through the infinite love of Christ, as Joshua 1:5 assures us.

Dear brothers and sisters, calling upon the name of Jesus is an extraordinary invitation to experience immeasurable power, unparalleled protection, and abundant provision that are available to us as believers. In Him, we find a towering fortress—a sanctuary where we discover refuge and comfort. As citizens of Zion, we have the profound privilege of living under the divine governance of heaven, undeterred by the ever-changing circumstances of this world.

REFLECTION

CHAPTER 40
THE PROMISE OF REST

"But now the LORD my God hath given me rest on every side, so that there is neither adversary nor evil occurrent."
1 Kings 5:4

Dear brothers and sisters in Christ, I bring you a message of hope and inspiration today. While the path of faith can be filled with difficulties and opponents, let us remember the unwavering faithfulness of our God. He has promised to give us rest on all sides and overcome our adversaries. Therefore, let our hearts rejoice and offer a resounding hallelujah!

In Psalm 109:29, David's plea for deliverance showcased his unwavering trust in God's justice. He earnestly prayed for his adversaries to be ashamed and confused. When we face opposition and encounter enemies, we can find comfort in knowing God sees everything. He is a just God who will not let the wickedness of our opponents prevail. In His perfect timing, He will establish justice and bring vindication to His beloved children.

In 1 Kings 5:4, King Solomon joyfully declares the goodness of the Lord and acknowledges the rest that God has bestowed upon him. This declaration echoes through time, reminding us that when we trust in the Lord, He grants us a divine peace that surpasses all understanding. Our God is not distant; He is a loving Father who deeply cares for His children. He sees the challenges and attacks we face and promises to be our refuge and strength in times of trouble.

So, what should we do when we face attacks? We should stand firm and not grow weary, even in the midst of adversity. As the apostle Paul proclaims in 2 Corinthians 4:16-18, though our outward bodies may perish, our inner spirit is renewed daily through the power of the Holy Spirit. The trials we face, no matter how burdensome, are temporary when viewed in light of eternity. God, in His wisdom, uses these challenges to refine us, strengthen our faith, and prepare us for an unimaginable glory in His eternal presence.

As we journey through life, we will inevitably encounter adversaries and confront various challenges. However, let us hold fast to the unchanging character of our faithful God, who will never leave us nor forsake us. In times of trouble, let us steadfastly fix our gaze on the eternal realm rather than the temporary circumstances that surround us. For in the kingdom of God, all adversaries will be defeated, and we will experience lasting peace, joy, and rest. Amen.

REFLECTION

ABOUT THE AUTHOR

Isaac Samuel II is a renowned pastor, author, bible scholar, public speaker, and the visionary founder of Check It Church International, a continuously growing ministry.

At an early age, Isaac Samuel II discovered the transformative power of faith and embarked on a lifelong journey of serving the Lord. At the age of seven, he began preaching and distributing evangelism tracts. As he grew, he became a dedicated cell and worship leader in his local church. In 2013, he took a bold step by establishing a pioneering church on the island of Cyprus, laying the foundation for his visionary venture, Check It Church International, which was founded in 2019. Since its inception, this online church has experienced remarkable growth, expanding from 75 followers to a vibrant community of over 22,000 individuals from more than 56 countries.

Isaac Samuel II's passion for evangelism has taken him across continents, where he has ministered and hosted impactful evangelism programs. His genuine desire to share the Gospel and inspire others to embrace a faith-filled life has touched countless lives worldwide.

In addition to his pastoral responsibilities, Isaac Samuel II serves as the CEO of Check It Clothing, a Christian apparel line. Through this venture, he encourages believers to boldly proclaim their faith and radiate God's love through their attire.

Isaac Samuel II's unwavering faith, dynamic preaching, and dedicated commitment to empowering believers have established him as a highly respected figure within the global Christian community. His ministry continues to transform lives, bringing people closer to God and inspiring them to live purposeful, transformed lives filled with faith.

www.ingramcontent.com/pod-product-compliance
Lightning Source LLC
Chambersburg PA
CBHW070710130626
46553CB00005B/1918